guitars
that shook
the world

A STAR-STUDDED COLLECTION OF THE WORLD'S MOST FAMOUS GUITARS

EDITED BY BRAD TOLINSKI, HAROLD STEINBLATT & TOM BEAUJOUR

HAL•LEONARD
CORPORATION

7777 W. BLUEMOUND RD. P.O. BOX 13819 MILWAUKEE, WI 53213

Published by HAL LEONARD CORPORATION
7777 West Bluemound Road
P.O. Box 13819
Milwaukee, Wisconsin 53213

Copyright © 1995 by HAL LEONARD CORPORATION

ISBN 0-7935-3488-7

Printed in the U.S.A.

ifags

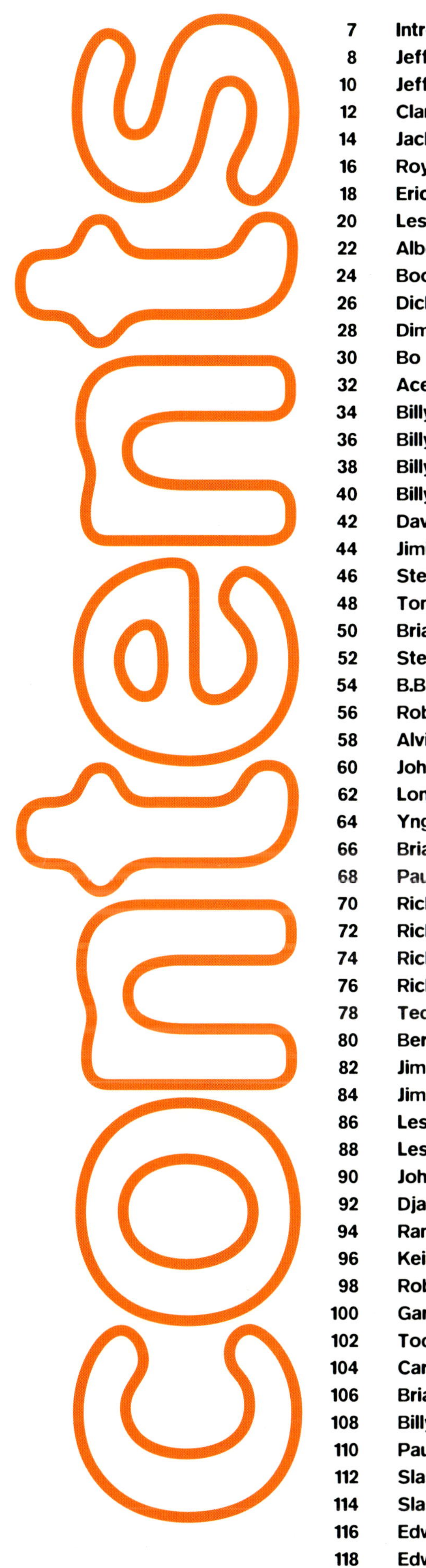

contents

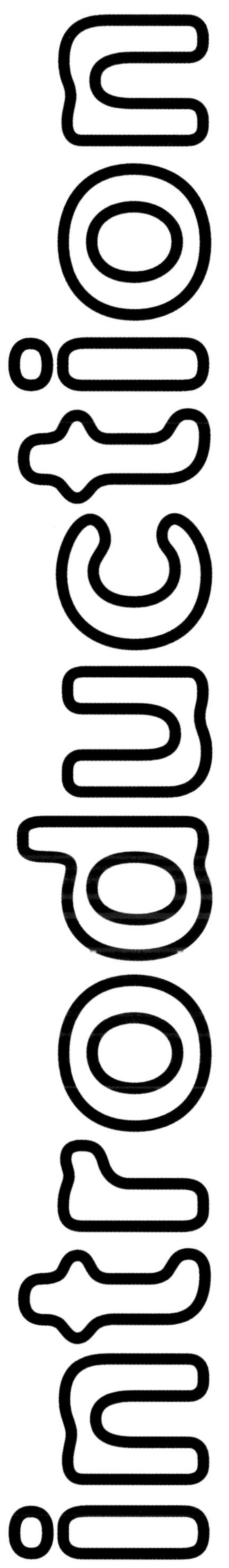

WHETHER IT'S THE howl of a bruised and battered '57 Fender Stratocaster or the shriek of a spanking new Gibson Les Paul, nothing screams rock and blues louder than the guitar. From the boogie-based rock and roll of the Fifties right down to the grunge revolution of the Nineties, the guitar has remained rock's single greatest icon. In fact, it is safe to say that no other instrument in modern times has inspired such loyalty, devotion, even obsession.

Why the guitar? There are a multitude of answers. Perhaps more than any other music, rock is about action and style—and no other musical instrument packs as much harmonic, melodic and rhythmic punch in such a portable, visually appealing package. The guitar is not only a powerful tool for self-expression, but also a versatile stage prop.

More than just an instrument, the guitar often becomes the extension of the musician's psyche. Some guitars become so closely associated with the artists who play them that it is almost impossible to think of them as separate entities: Stevie Ray Vaughan and his beloved "Number One" Strat, Johnny Ramone and his trusty white Mosrite, Brian May and his homemade Red Special—these are but a few of the dynamic duos that immediately come to mind.

It is this special kinship—this link between musician and instrument—that we celebrate in the volume that you now hold in your hands.

In the following pages, we, the editors of *Guitar World* magazine, have assembled the ultimate "hall of fame" guitar collection. These guitars—which originally appeared as "Collector's Choice" centerfolds in *Guitar World*—have achieved special notoriety because of their genuinely historic connection with some of the greatest rock and blues players.

Over 50 immortal electric and acoustic axes are presented here in glorious color portraits taken by some of rock's finest photographers. The photos are accompanied by informative text relating the background of the instruments—in many instances including anecdotes supplied by their celebrity owners.

More than mere collectibles, these six-stringed icons have changed the face of modern music and culture—truly, guitars that shook the world.

Brad Tolinski
Editor-in-Chief
Guitar World

jeff beck's
FENDER ESQUIRE

AMONG THIS ESQUIRE'S claims to fame is that it is the first guitar ever to be recorded feeding back. The train sounds and the sliding, shrieking guitar parts Jeff Beck played on the Yardbirds' "Heart Full Of Soul" and "Train Kept A Rollin'" were all squeezed from this instrument.

According to pickup baron Seymour Duncan, the Esquire's current owner, Jeff Beck acquired the guitar for $60 in 1964 from John Maus, of the Sixties pop-rock band the Walker Brothers. Maus had carved a contour in the Esquire's ash body to give it the look of a Stratocaster. Beck played the guitar regularly for the next 10 years and got the most for his $60 as he established himself as one of the all-time greats of rock guitar. The Esquire was also used by Jimmy Page at certain performances during his tenure with the Yardbirds.

Beck destroyed several necks while the guitar was in his possession; the current neck was made in 1956 (the body is a '54). In February of 1974, Beck presented this guitar as a gift to Seymour Duncan, who has kept the Esquire in the exact condition he received it.

photo by kevin westenberg

A serial number of dubious authenticity suggests that the guitar may have been made in 1952, but the tuners are replacements, as are the pickups—even the neck was made later than the body. Though the guitar's refinish looks black, it is, in fact, very dark brown—a color Beck describes as "oxblood."

This Les Paul, which Beck most likely bought in the early Seventies, was the third such Gibson that he owned. His first, a 1959 sunburst model, was stolen from him in New York in the late Sixties. The second began life as a sunburst, but Beck stripped it down to the natural wood; he used it on songs like "Hi Ho Silver Lining" (1967) and "Barabajagal" (1969).

By the time he recorded *Blow By Blow*, Jeff was already shifting his allegiance to Fender. As he recalls, "There was also a '58 Strat on that record, and a Telecaster with Gibson humbuckers that I got in trade for my Yardbirds '54 Esquire. It was only later that I realized what I'd done. I shouldn't have let that guitar go!" Fortunately, Jeff still owns this historic Les Paul.

clarence "gatemouth" brown's
GIBSON FIREBIRD

"I BOUGHT THIS guitar almost brand-new in a Denver pawnshop in 1966," says multi-instrumentalist, multi-stylist Texas bluesman Clarence "Gatemouth" Brown. "Two years later I was living in Durango, Colorado, and a leather craftsman who was a friend of mine asked if he could borrow the guitar. When he returned it the next morning, it had the leather pickguard on it. Ever since then, i've just cherished the guitar. It became my number one instrument and a trademark of sorts."

Brown has had several "number one" guitars. At the beginning of his career, more than 45 years ago, he played a Gibson L-5. He later moved on to Telecasters before finally settling on the Firebird. "It's a great guitar," says Brown. "It stays in tune, it's light and it's got great drive—the pickups are real hot."

According to Ron Harris, Brown's tour manager, rhythm guitarist and "emergency luthier," the Firebird was completely overhauled by Heritage Guitars in 1987. "They refretted it, refinished it, put a new tailpiece on—it had a whammy—put in Bill Lawrence pickups, removed the Schaller tuning heads and replaced them with Gibsons and added a Tune-O-Matic bridge. They did a great job."

photo by lorinda sullivan

MUSIC MAN
GATEMOUTH
212-HD

jack bruce's
GIBSON EB-0 BASS

THE THIRD ELECTRIC bass to be introduced by Gibson, the EB-0 first appeared in 1959 and quickly became the company's most popular model. The SG-shaped version was introduced in 1961 and remained in the catalog until 1972. The EB-0 pictured here is particularly noteworthy because it was owned by two important bassists, Jack Bruce and the late Felix Pappalardi, of Mountain fame. Here is Bruce's explanation of how he came to acquire the instrument, which is inscribed, "To Jack, XXX, Felix":

"Felix and I worked very closely together on the production of Cream recordings, starting with the second album, *Disraeli Gears*," Bruce recalls. "We became very close friends, and he also produced my first solo album, *Songs For The Tailor*, in London. Felix then went on to form the wonderful band Mountain, with Leslie West. I first heard that band when I was a member of Lifetime, with Tony Williams, Larry Young and John McLaughlin, and we opened for Mountain. This was a revelation for me, especially the beautiful warmth of Leslie's tone and Felix's incredibly deep bass sound. That is the sound of the EB-0.

"In those days I was still playing my beloved EB-3," Bruce continues, "but Felix got down on the floor of the dressing room, carved his name on the EB-0 bass and just gave it to me with a hug. He made a great contribution to the music we love, and I for one will never forget him."

photo by john peden

Gibson
Man To Jack XXX FELIX

roy buchanan's
FENDER TELECASTER

IT WAS THE influence of B.B. King that led Roy Buchanan to name his 1953 Telecaster "Nancy." According to Buchanan's widow, Judy, "Roy must have named the guitar around 1955, when B.B. King started getting popular. B.B. had named *his* guitar 'Lucille,' and Roy thought that was a cool thing to do. So he called the Telecaster 'Nancy.' The name has no special significance, as far as I know."

While this instrument is now a highly prized vintage collectible, the Telecaster was still a newfangled oddity when Roy Buchanan bought one back in 1953. The guitar's forerunner was the Broadcaster, which Fender had developed in the late Forties. The Broadcaster name was soon changed to Telecaster due to a trademark conflict, but the instrument itself remained essentially unchanged.

Nancy's butterscotch color is the result of the guitar's constant exposure to cigarette smoke and other oxidants. A peek under the Bakelite pickguard reveals the original light blonde see-through finish. Marks on the body behind the bridge are vestiges of intonation adjustments, and the hole just under the B string is testament to a botched midnight attempt at producing a string bender. "That guitar had been everywhere and through everything," says Ms. Buchanan.

Although he occasionally flirted with Gibsons, Buchanan remained faithful to the Telecaster throughout his largely unsung career. Only towards the end of his life did Roy retire this guitar from the road, "because," says Ms. Buchanan, "he treasured it so much."

eric clapton's
GIBSON LES PAUL

AT FIRST GLANCE, this Gibson Les Paul appears less than impressive. It has a non-standard red finish (pointing to the likelihood that it was refinished at some point), as well as a serial number that has been rewritten in the wrong typeface and with a hyphen that instruments of that period never had, making it impossible to date accurately. Furthermore, neither the machine heads nor the truss-rod cover are original.

But this Les Paul doesn't just sing like any other—it weeps. Eric Clapton used this axe for his now-legendary solo on the Beatles' "While My Guitar Gently Weeps," on the *White Album*. Shortly after that 1968 recording session, Clapton gave the guitar to George Harrison, who still owns it today.

Serious vintage collectors may frown at it, but for Beatles and Clapton fans, this guitar holds an important place in history.

les claypool's
CARL THOMPSON SIX-STRING FRETLESS BASS

"IT SCARED THE hell out of me at first, but I soon learned to love it." So says Les Claypool of the outsized six-string fretless that was custom-built for him by veteran luthier Carl Thompson. The behemoth bass boasts a 36-inch scale length. "Anything less," asserts Thompson, "and you're just getting a semblance of a low B." He ought to know, since he built what was arguably the world's first six-string bass, for session player Anthony Jackson, back in 1974—the same year he also built the first-ever piccolo bass for Stanley Clarke.

The Brooklyn-based craftsman went all-out on Claypool's bass. The laminate "rainbow" body contains strips of walnut, curly maple, padauk, purple heart, ebony and cocobolo. The three-dimensional carved body scroll is something of a Thompson trademark, as is the body extension on the end. Rather than passing through the body, the strings are threaded through the back of this rear extension—near the strap pin. They're stretched over a one-piece handmade wooden bridge and anchored by Schaller tuning machines.

The neck is a laminate creature, too. The basic part is made of quartersawn hard rock maple. The center of the fingerboard is of Indian ebony, with one-eighth-inch-wide strips of padauk, cocobolo and ebony on either side. "I usually use the day I finish the bass as a serial number," says Thompson, "and I just happened to finish this one on my birthday. So its serial number is 2-5-90."

The instrument was completed just in time for Primus' *Sailing The Seas Of Cheese*, on which Les played it extensively. It also figures prominently on *Miscellaneous Debris* and *Pork Soda*.

albert collins'
NDER TELECASTER

WHEN BLUES GREAT **Albert Collins' 1965 Telecaster was stolen in the late Sixties, Fender presented him with a replacement—a new Thinline Tele. Apparently, that guitar left Collins cold, for he subsequently traded it for the blonde 1961 guitar shown here. It became the main instrument for the man who earned the nickname "the Ice Man" for his peculiar ability to send cold chills up the spines of his listeners (as well as for such classic instrumentals as "The Freeze" and "Frosty").**

Atypically, this Telecaster has a humbucking pickup in the neck position—a state of affairs that already existed when Collins bought the guitar. He had the Tele refinished and added white binding to the guitar's front and back. There is little fretboard wear and tear below the middle of the neck, a byproduct of Collins' unique style: besides tuning the guitar to an F minor chord, he usually capoed the neck at the fifth fret and above.

This guitar served as the blueprint for the Fender Signature Model Telecaster that bore Collins' name.

bootsy collins'
SPACE BASS

WHEN WARNER BROS. called Bootsy Collins to arrange a cover photo for his Rubber Band's 1976 debut album, *Stretching Out*, the funkateer had a mild panic attack. His new bass, it seems, was still under construction. Not just any old four-string twanger, the Space Bass was the realization of Bootsy's personal vision: he had drawn up the plans himself.

Recalls Bootsy: "I'm like, 'Wow! The bass is not ready yet. *I've gotta have the bass on the cover!*" Bootsy explained the situation to his luthier ("a kid named Larry Pless who worked in the back of a Detroit accordion store"), and the two of them devised a scheme. "When you look at the album, if you really look at the bass, it's not finished at all. Larry just painted on fake pickups, and the tuning pegs are just little pieces of metal we stuck on the headstock."

Even when he had the genuine, working article in hand, Bootsy's troubles were far from over. Soon after the Space Bass had attained some notoriety of its own, it was stolen after a gig in Chicago. "During that time, people were coming in to see the star glasses, the Bootsy, *and* the Space Bass, you know? So I had to call Larry Pless and get a second one."

A year later, the original turned up unscathed. Never the vengeful type, Bootsy didn't bother to find out who had taken it. "But the ones who found him said that everywhere he took it, people were like, 'That's Bootsy's bass!' So he couldn't sell it; he couldn't do nothin'. It made him very sad."

These days, when the funkiest resident of outer space isn't playing his number one bass, he keeps it chained up in his hotel room. And don't even think about asking him to play it. "I tell people, 'If you can't play it, you can't play *with* it. And besides, my bass don't play for nobody but me!' It's a jealous kind of thing."

dick dale's

FENDER STRATOCASTER ("THE BEAST")

"I'VE ONLY HAD the one guitar all my life," says Dick Dale of this battle-scarred left-handed Strat, nicknamed "The Beast." The guitar has served the self-proclaimed "King of Surf Guitar" faithfully on every track he has ever cut, from his 1961 debut single, "Let's Go Trippin'," to his latest album, *Unknown Territory*. The Beast is one tough animal; most guitars would be reduced to kindling by the more than three decades of use and abuse the Strat has suffered at Dale's hands.

According to John English of the Fender Custom Shop, who went over this guitar with a fine-toothed comb while he was designing the Dick Dale Signature Stratocaster, the Beast was built in 1960. The original electronics have long since been modified to suit Dale's needs: an extra switch instantly engages the neck/middle pickup combination regardless of what the five-way switch is set to, and all of the pots, except for one volume control, have been removed. Dale strings the guitar upside down with super-heavy, bridge cable-like .014–.060's.

Although the guitar used to be sunburst, Dale claims to have refinished it at least nine times in order to foil would-be copycats who, during the guitarist's early-Sixties heyday, would paint their guitars to look just like his. "I used to go in and have it painted every week, just to be cute," Dale grins. "Finally my buddy, who used to paint cars, painted it the first metal gold-flake." Dale subsequently attached two decals to the guitar: an American flag on the top horn and a Kenpo Karate emblem, which he received from his martial arts instructor.

photo by karjean ng

dimebag darrell's

"THE BLUE DEAN'S got a *cool* story, man!" crows Dimebag Darrell. But what else would you expect from Pantera's red-hot cowboy from hell?

"My dad bought me my first Dean for Christmas," explains Darrell. "I broke his ass for it—it cost him $1,100. He really had to go out of his way to afford that for me. But I was dying to have one, and he fixed me up. For that I'll be forever grateful to him. But not two weeks later, I won another Dean in a guitar playing contest.

"I was thrilled to have two Deans, but I was 16 and I really needed a car. So I decided to sell one of the guitars, to raise money for some wheels. I didn't want to bum my dad out, so I sold the contest guitar for $600—even though I liked it better than the one he bought me for Christmas."

Darrell's contest guitar floated around and eventually made its way into the hands of noted Texas six-string expert Buddy Blaze, who worked at Kramer guitars. Blaze liked the guitar so much that he had it custom-painted blue and added the axe's now-legendary lightning bolts.

"One day I was hanging out in this music store and saw Buddy's blue Dean, and I flipped," continues Darrell. "All I could say was, 'Who the hell owns that guitar, man? I want to buy it!' But because of the radical paint job, I didn't know that it was actually the guitar that I had sold. Anyway, he wouldn't sell it to me.

"Later, I got to know Buddy, and he was going to put together a new guitar for me in exchange for the Gibson Flying V that I had. I gave him the V, and a month went by and Buddy just couldn't seem to find the time to put the axe together for me. One day he showed up on my doorstep with a box. I opened it up, and inside was the blue Dean. He said, 'Dude, it was your prize to begin with. Here you go.'"

In addition to the custom paint job, Darrell's Dean features a Floyd Rose licensed locking system and a Bill Lawrence L-500-XL pickup. "In many ways, my bridge-position Lawrence is really the key to my sound," reports Dimebag. "It's a killer pickup. On the treble strings, it's a bitch—sounds almost like you're running it through a Crybaby wah with the pedal pushed down. And, of course, it's real thick and chunky on the low strings."

bo diddley's
HOMEMADE GUITAR

Long before Edward Van Halen demonstrated that a great rock guitarist could also be a great rock-guitar *designer*, there was Elias McDaniel, better known as Bo Diddley. McDaniel, who gained worldwide fame as the father of the "Bo Diddley beat" and as the composer of "I'm A Man," "Who Do You Love" and other rock and roll classics, built this guitar back in 1945. The shape of this acoustic instrument (which he electrified in 1955) clearly presages the custom-made rectangular guitars for which he later became celebrated.

photo by john peden

BO DIDDLEY
IN THE SPOTLIGHT
CHECKER LP 2976
BO DIDDLEY is a GUNSLINGER
CHECKER LP 2977
FIN' WITH
LEY
To
BO DIDDLEY
CHECKER LP 2982
LEY'S
CHECKER LP 2983
From Otha man BO DIDDLEY
MADE BY E MS BO DIDDLEY 1945
To THE HARD ROCK 1992 With Love
BO DIDDLEY IS A....
CHECKER LP 2980
CHECKER LP 2985
BO- DIDDLEY & company

ace frehley's
GIBSON LES PAUL CUSTOM

PRIOR TO CUSTOMIZING this Custom, Ace Frehley ruined at least one guitar in his quest to create the ultimate smoking love gun. "On the first or second Kiss tour, I got really loaded and put a smoke bomb in the volume-control box of my tobacco sunburst Standard," recalls Frehley. "I had the fuse hanging out from the back plate, and I lit it right before my guitar solo. The smoke oozed out from both pickups, and the people went nuts. I thought it looked great, too, but it completely destroyed all my volume and tone pots."

Following the demise of his Standard, Frehley brought a Les Paul Custom to a designer who customized the instrument so that it would belch smoke without suffering any ill effects. "There's an asbestos-covered metal box under the rhythm pickup," says Ace, "a battery pack that jettisons the smoke bomb and a halogen lamp to make the guitar look like it's on fire—though it does catch fire half the time. I never used my rhythm pickup anyway, so I converted its volume and tone knobs to trigger the smoke and light. There's also a trap door in the pickup that drops out so you can see the light."

Frehley has used this guitar night in and night out since he had it customized some 17 years ago, and all those explosions have, of course, taken their toll on the instrument. "The neck has had to be reinforced a number of times because the metal box really heats up. The larger the venue, the more smoke bombs I put in, and the more damage it can do to the neck. It's been straightened a few times, refretted a few times, and a new fretboard was put in. But the guitar has held up, and it still sings. I still record and tour with it."

While the smoke bombs have indeed caused some damage to the guitar, Frehley has been more concerned with his own health than with that of the instrument: "The first few times I tried it, the back of the guitar got so hot it burned a hole in my costume and burned my leg. After I ruined a few costumes, we covered it with asbestos so I wouldn't get burned. I still get burned sometimes—I just try to keep it away from my crotch."

photo by lorinda sullivan

billy gibbons'
CUSTOM GIBSON LONE STAR

IN MUCH THE same way that Brian Wilson and the Beach Boys created the "California myth," ZZ Top have fashioned a magical landscape out of their home state, Texas. What more natural expression of guitarist Billy Gibbons' love for Texas than for him to commission Gibson to custom-build an instrument shaped exactly like the Lone Star State itself!

The guitar's body and neck are made of mahogany; the fingerboard is of rosewood. Of special interest is an active circuit that, like those featured in Gibson's RD line, consists of a compressor/expander. The guitar also includes special switches, recessed in the back of the instrument, that activate the effects. Gibbons describes these easily accessible extra switches as being "right behind El Paso." In keeping with the aesthetic simplicity of the guitar's face, these are concealed.

Other features are a battery pack ("located near Austin") and a headstock sporting a lone star that passes right through the Gibson logo. There is also a brass plate on the back, commemorating the presentation of the instrument to Billy, and a brass truss-rod cover with the word "TEXAS" engraved on it.

Designed and constructed by C.E. Burge, this guitar is reportedly the last instrument made in the Gibson factory in Kalamazoo, Michigan, before the company relocated to Nashville.

According to Billy, the guitar is "very loud, with tremendous sustain. Of course, it has a sound as big as Texas."

billy gibbons'
CUSTOMIZED FENDER JAGUAR

"BELIEVE IT OR not," says Billy Gibbons, "we still have a Jag lurking in our stable. This particular instrument is the second guitar I ever owned and can be heard on 'PCH,' off *Antenna*. There's a VU meter where the neck pickup probably would have existed. Also, this guitar features a painting of a Rick surfboard. I don't know what that has to do with anything, but it's there."

photo by james bland

billy gibbons'
"MUDDYWOOD" GUITAR

THIS UNUSUAL GUITAR, designed by Billy Gibbons with Rich Rayburn, of Memphis Guitars, is literally a piece of blues history, for the source of the wood from which the guitar is built is none other than the cabin Muddy Waters grew up in, on the Stovall plantation, near Clarksdale, Mississippi.

Gibbons decided to build the guitar after he and his fellow ZZ Toppers visited the cabin prior to touring the Delta Blues Museum in Clarksdale. The building was a shambles, thanks to a recent tornado. "The Mississippi State Department had asked the Stovall family to dismantle it," says Gibbons, "because they thought it might be a safety hazard."

It occurred to Gibbons to take a large roof beam from the cabin as a souvenir. Later, as he and his companions returned to Memphis, they had a truly inspired brainstorm: "It dawned on us to have a guitar fashioned out of this piece of wood. In all of about 15 minutes, we sketched out the body. The paint scheme, of course, is intended to represent the winding, meandering Mississippi River, culminating at the triangular-shaped headstock, which is representative of the Delta. The candy-copper finish is reminiscent of the flavor of the mighty, muddy Mississippi, and the river-squiggle design is highlighted by a grass-green pinstripe. Once they started sawing into this beam, I was cussed a number of ways. There were knot holes, worm holes, nails, water warps—it was just a real untame piece of timber to be reckoned with. When it was completed, one simple pickup was added and it was just a burner. The damn thing sounds good."

After the Muddywood's world tour of Hard Rock Cafés in 1988, the guitar was donated by ZZ Top to the Delta Blues Museum, "to pay homage to this American art form."

billy gibbons'

CUSTOM PEAVEY "VIVA LAS VEGAS" MODEL

In Billy Gibbons' own words, "The 'Viva Las Vegas' guitar was created in Meridian, Mississippi, where you can throw dice or go by the Peavey specialty guitar shop and say, 'Hey, make me a "Viva Las Vegas" guitar!' It plays quite well, by the way. The hardware was a gift from an actual slot machine."

VIVA LAS MEGA$
BAR
BAR
BAR
7
7
25¢
PEAVEY

david gilmour's
FENDER STRATOCASTER #0001

THOUGH THIS STRATOCASTER, owned by Pink Floyd's David Gilmour, bears the serial number 0001, it is *not* the very first Strat ever made. Contrary to popular belief, Fender's serial numbers are not sequential. Nevertheless, this guitar was certainly manufactured by Fender in Fullerton, California, in 1954, the first year of the Strat's long and illustrious production history.

No clear picture has emerged as to exactly when in 1954 the Strat was launched, but it appears to have been between March and May. Gilmour's guitar is dated June 1954 on its neck joint. What probably happened was that this Strat was made for a special customer—it has an unusual custom-color finish, and the hardware was given non-standard gold plating—and someone decided to make it even more special by topping it off with a one-off serial number.

Whatever its true origins, this is a very nice early Strat, one which Gilmour clearly cherishes. "Some guitars make everyone sound the same," he says. "Others tend to emphasize the differences—which this one does. I haven't got a clue what it's worth. But it's not for sale."

jimi hendrix'
GIBSON FLYING V

Back when it first appeared in 1958, the radically shaped Gibson Flying V represented an extreme departure for a manufacturer famous for the austerity of its designs. Introduced along with two other futuristic guitars—the Explorer and the Moderne (the latter of which apparently never got off the drawing board)—the Flying V and its companions were commercial flops during their original issue.

But designer Ted McCarty had the last laugh in the late Sixties when rock and blues guitarists such as Albert King, Dave Davies of the Kinks and, of course, Jimi Hendrix discovered and popularized the model now universally known for its stinging tone and tail-fin good looks.

The '68–'69 version of the V differs from its '58 counterpart in several respects. The korina body of the original was replaced in the Sixties by one made of mahogany, and the string-through-body, boomerang-shaped tailpiece was eliminated in favor of a Gibson "Maestro Vibrola." Also worth noting is the "triangle" control-knob scheme, as opposed to the "three-in-a-row" layout of the Fifties version.

Jimi's one-of-a-kind model took this one step further. Custom-ordered from Manny's, the famed New York music store, the guitar features a black finish, gold-plated hardware and the split-diamond fingerboard inlay usually found on Gibson's Trini Lopez models.

Although primarily associated with the Fender Stratocaster, Jimi Hendrix often relied on the V for blues performances, particularly of the Chicago blues-style "Red House."

steve howe's

GIBSON ES-175D

STEVE HOWE TURNED the heads of many of his fellow guitarists in the early Sixties by using what was widely regarded as a jazz guitar in a blues and rock format. He bought this classic Gibson ES-175D in 1964, when he was performing in a London-based blues group called the Syndicats. Howe continued to use the 175 in his next three bands—Tomorrow, a short-lived outfit called Bodast and finally in Yes.

"Although my first electric guitars were a Guyatone and a Burns Jazz, the ES-175D was my first Gibson guitar and represented the start of a long love affair with Gibsons," says Howe. The guitarist used this particular ES model throughout his celebrated career with Yes—one of the most adventurous progressive rock groups of the Seventies. Howe used this classic instrument on such standout Yes tracks as "Heart Of The Sunrise" (*Fragile*, 1971) and for the final solo in "Siberian Khatru" (*Close To The Edge*, 1972).

Howe fondly remembers the time Bodast played a support to Chuck Berry at the Royal Albert Hall, in London, in 1969. "I got a chance to ask Chuck what he thought of my 175," Steve recalls. "He picked it up, strummed it a bit, and said, 'This is great, a lovely guitar.' So I put the guitar back in the case and felt really good. Chuck Berry played my guitar!"

tony iommi's
GIBSON SG

"I BOUGHT MY Gibson SG in a music store in Birmingham, England, back in 1967," says Black Sabbath's Tony Iommi. "I was told it was a '64, but I've never verified that. Originally it was my backup guitar—my primary guitar was a Fender Stratocaster. While I was recording the first track on our first album, the Strat's pickups blew. I couldn't find anyone who knew how to repair it, and we didn't have replacement parts in those days, so I just trashed it and started using the SG. It sounded good, so I never looked back. It was my primary guitar on *Black Sabbath*, *Paranoid* and *Master Of Reality*."

Iommi did little to alter the SG during the years he recorded Sabbath's classic trilogy. Later, however, he customized the Gibson with the aid of guitar-maker John Birch. "I replaced the bridge pickup with a hand-wound John Birch humbucker," Iommi explains. "Birch was a craftsman who designed and modified guitars for me when companies refused to meet my demands. Besides winding custom pickups for my instruments, he also built my first 24-fret guitar when others said it was impossible."

The cherry-colored, fire-breathing axe has been spending its golden years in the mustachioed metal master's closet, though Iommi does pull it out from time to time. "I still use it in the studio occasionally," he says. "My biggest problem with the instrument is that it has a very weak neck. It actually goes out of tune as much as a half step if you apply too much pressure on it."

brian jones'

VOX MARK VI

THE LATE, LEGENDARY Brian Jones will forever be linked with his white teardrop Vox Mark VI. One of the most recognizable instruments in rock history, Jones' distinctively shaped guitar became familiar to millions thanks to the Rolling Stones' many appearances on "The Ed Sullivan Show," "Shindig," "Hullabaloo," and other television programs in the mid Sixties.

While the standard version of the Mark VI had three pickups, Jones' guitar, which was most likely built in 1964, is one of only five two-pickup models produced by Vox. Other features include a metal pickguard, a copy of a Strat bridge and, for easy access to the control cavity (and like some Gretsches), detachable back pads.

Brian Jones' Mark VI is now permanently on display at the New York City branch of the Hard Rock Café, which purchased the guitar at auction from Sotheby's in 1984.

photo by john peden

steve jones'
GIBSON LES PAUL CUSTOM

To GUITARISTS, THIS cream-colored early-Seventies Les Paul Custom is nothing less than the Holy Grail of Punk. Once owned by legendary New York Doll proto-punk Syl Sylvain, it eventually made its way into the hands of Sex Pistol Steve Jones. Jones used this stripped-down Gibson and a Fender Twin Reverb—the latter heisted from the back of Bob Marley and the Wailers' equipment truck—to detonate "Anarchy In The U.K." and other classics from the revolutionary *Never Mind The Bollocks, Here's The Sex Pistols*.

The Les Paul's original creamy white finish has faded to a smoke-and-sweat-stained yellow. The knobs and machine heads have been replaced; the originals were destroyed in various flights of six-string recklessness. The kitschy Forties pinup stickers with which Sylvain decorated the guitar have become worn with age, while two telltale screw holes are all that remain of a pickguard.

Jones, who recently sold the guitar in order to pay for repairs on his Harley-Davidson motorcycle, is not big on sentimentality. "That stuff don't mean much. I've got a couple more Pauls. It's nothing; I've even sold gold records before. As long as I get to play rock and roll— that's all I care about."

Gibson
GOD S   QUEEN
STEVIE JONES

b.b. king's
GIBSON CUSTOM SHOP "LUCILLE"

B.B. KING HAS bestowed the name "Lucille" on every guitar he's owned since the day in 1949 when he rushed into a burning club in Twist, Arkansas, to rescue a favorite intrument. The blaze had been set by two men arguing over a woman named Lucille, and King immortalized her to remind himself how foolish he'd been to risk his life. In 1980, Gibson added fire to the bluesman's own immortality by introducing the B.B. King Standard and the B.B. King Custom, both based on the ES-355, the Gibson model favored by King. The ES-355 was discontinued in 1982 and the Standard discontinued in 1985, and in 1988 the Custom was officially renamed "Lucille."

The Gibson Lucille differs in several ways from the original ES-355. The primary difference is that it has a solid top, while the 355 had f-holes. Also, where the 355 had a vibrato, the Lucille uses a TP-6 fine-tuning tailpiece. In terms of electronics, the Lucille utilizes Gibson's 490R and 490T pickups. It has two volume and two tone controls, as well as a six-way "Vari-tone" switch, which allows the player to progressively "dry" the tone, giving him the potential for 18 different sounds. The Lucille has two output jacks: one mono and one stereo that gives each pickup its own channel.

King's guitar was built for him by Gibson in 1993. The differences between B.B.'s Lucille and an off-the-rack model are primarily cosmetic; King's guitar features his name inlaid with abalone on the neck, along with two abalone guitars. Also, the Custom Lucille has a flip-out string crank built into the button of each key, for ease of tuning.

robbie krieger's
GIBSON LES PAUL CUSTOM

"I PAID A guy named Rocky $400 for this guitar in 1968," says Robbie Krieger of his 1955 Les Paul Custom. "That was a helluva lot of money at the time. I thought it was gorgeous, and I intended to make it my number one instrument, replacing my SG. But it has a neck like a telephone pole, and I just couldn't get comfortable with it. Instead, I set it up for slide—I put a high nut on and raised the action way up."

From 1968's *Waiting For The Sun*, the Doors' third album, until the group's demise, Krieger used this black beauty for all his studio and stage slide work. The guitar was featured on "Hello, I Love You," "Been Down So Long" and the intro to "L.A. Woman," among other songs. Krieger employed both open G and open D tunings, so he equipped the guitar with banjo-style tuners which allowed him to retune with one turn of the pegs. He continued using the guitar for slide even after removing the tuners, which broke repeatedly. "They were a good idea," Krieger says, "and they were great when they worked. But they couldn't really handle the tension of guitar strings."

Though he uses a Gibson 355 almost exclusively now, Krieger still cherishes the Les Paul. "It's a great instrument, but I have to say that I'm not even sure that it's a '55," he says. "It definitely is one of the first model years, because it has two single-coils. [*Gibson began equipping the Les Pauls with humbuckers in 1957.*] The only reason I didn't put a humbucker in is I didn't even know the difference at the time. I left the pickups alone until about 10 years ago, when the bass one died, and I replaced it with a Seymour Duncan."

alvin lee's
GIBSON ES-335

BLUES ROCKER AND pioneer shredder Alvin Lee is best known for the extended, show-stopping version of "I'm Going Home" he and his band Ten Years After played at the original Woodstock festival in 1969. He used this Gibson ES-335 at Woodstock—and on everything from Ten Years After's 1967 debut to his 1994 solo album, *I Hear You Rocking* (Viceroy).

"I bought 'Big Red' in 1963 when I was 18 for 45 pounds, case included," the British guitarist says. "I'd always wanted an American guitar—that was the Holy Grail—and I especially wanted a Gibson ever since I saw Chuck Berry and [*Elvis Presley's lead guitarist*] Scotty Moore playing them.

"When I bought the guitar, the pickup configuration was normal, but I immediately took the covers off to give it a little more kick and top end—I've always been an amateur boffin [*tech*]. I liked the Fender sound and always thought it would be great to have a half-and-half guitar, so eventually I put in a middle Strat pickup, which has a nice hollow sound. I also put on a TP-6 tailpiece with fine tuning as soon as they came out."

Lee's Woodstock triumph established his reputation—and gave Big Red one of its more prominent "tattoos."

"When I was on stage at the festival, a Woodstock sticker somehow got passed to me while I was playing and I just slapped it on. The peace stickers came to me in a very similar manner in 1967 at the Fillmore West, in San Francisco, and the rest just somehow appeared. In 1973 I broke the neck off, and when they replaced it, they also relacquered the guitar, so the stickers became permanent fixtures, which is fine."

TEN YEARS LATER
TEN YEAR
TYL
AMERICA'S DAIRYLAND
TYA 69
JAN WISCONSIN 83

john lennon's
RICKENBACKER 325

THE BEATLES' AUGUST 1965 performance at Shea Stadium ranks among the most famous rock concerts in history. Though most of the audience couldn't hear the music above the screams and general hysteria that persisted throughout the show, they could at least see the Beatles—and John Lennon's black Rickenbacker 325. Beatles fans can now see that guitar once more, as well as other Beatles memorabilia never before exhibited publically in the United States, at the Rock and Roll Hall of Fame in Cleveland.

Lennon bought his first Rickenbacker 325 in 1960, when the Beatles went to play in Hamburg, Germany. After using that guitar extensively on stage and in the studio, he was given this guitar, his second 325, by Rickenbacker when the Beatles first came to America in 1964. This model featured a new vibrato bar and a five-knob control layout. Lennon first played his new 325 in public during the Beatles' second appearance on "The Ed Sullivan Show," broadcast live from the Deauville Hotel in Miami, Florida. The guitar was first used in the studio on "Can't Buy Me Love," recorded a few weeks later.

photo courtesy of the rock and roll hall of fame

lonnie mack's
GIBSON FLYING V

LONNIE MACK WAS **one of the fewer than 100 guitarists to purchase the Flying V when Gibson introduced it in 1958, and he's been identified with it ever since. His road-tested axe, despite more than a few trips to the repair shop, still boasts many of the stock features of the debut V: the slight squaring off at the neck/body joint, two P.A.F. humbucking pickups with a three-way selector switch, gold-plated hardware and two tone controls and a master volume knob all in a row. The custom-designed Bigsby vibrato assembly is unique.**

Mack once broke the neck off at the heel. "I was doing a Bo Diddley song at a Florida roadhouse in '66 or '67," he recalls. "I used to play it with my toes, bottles, mike stands, anything I could pick up. So I was down on the floor with a 50-foot cord and I broke the neck off. I took the guitar and threw it in the trash can."

Mack later recovered the guitar and had it repaired. In 1963 the V was refinished in the SG cherry style seen here. The leopard skin gris-gris bag attached to the guitar strap contains guitar picks, coins and other "essentials."

yngwie malmsteen's
FENDER STRATOCASTER ("THE DUCK")

THIS 1972 STRATOCASTER, nicknamed "The Duck" by Yngwie Malmsteen, is certainly the most celebrated of the neoclassical pioneer's guitars. "I was in Japan last year for a big music convention," he says, "and while I was signing autographs, lots of fans asked me to sign guitars that were total copies of this one—right down to the Donald Duck sticker on the headstock, the 'Play Loud' sticker on the body, and the Ferrari decal on the back."

Like most of Yngwie's Strats, this one is fitted with DiMarzio HS-3 pickups in the bridge and neck positions, with the original pickup still in the middle, and the standard Fender bridge. The maple fingerboard was scalloped by Yngwie himself in 1980. In 1987, while playing "Queen In Love" in Anchorage, Alaska, Yngwie and his guitar had an unforgettable experience: "An over-enthusiastic fan threw a half-empty one-liter bottle of Jack Daniels onstage and hit the seventeenth fret so hard, it popped right out of the wood!" Yngwie subsequently had the guitar refretted with Dunlop 6000 frets.

Yngwie bought the guitar in the late Seventies, in his native Sweden, from a drummer auditioning for his band. This Strat has appeared on the cover of numerous Malmsteen albums and is the guitar he used to play all the solos on his Grammy-nominated *Yngwie J. Malmsteen's Rising Force* (Polydor, 1984). "It's not my favorite Strat," says Yngwie, "but for some reason it's one of my best-sounding ones. It's been my main guitar since '78. I used it 99 percent of the time in Steeler and Alcatrazz, and I've played it on all my tours. I'm retiring it from road work this year. I don't want it to get stolen or more beaten to death than it already is! This puppy's been through a lot, from constant use and abuse onstage—the headstock has broken off at least six times, and I used to put my cigarettes out on it all the time.

"I'm not very kind to my instruments. Sometimes I'll throw my guitar high into the air, but a spotlight may get in my eyes when I try to catch it. So rather than let the guitar break my hand, I let it crash onto the floor."

Fender STRATOCASTER
PLAY LOUD

brian may's
RED SPECIAL

BRIAN MAY DESIGNED and built his Red Special guitar when he was a teenager, and it has been his main guitar ever since. He played it on every Queen album and tour, as well as on numerous side projects and his solo album *Back To The Light*.

Brian and his dad began work on the Red Special in 1962 and took two years to complete it. "I was 17 when it was finished," he recalls. "I knew I wanted a guitar that would sing and have warmth to it, but also a nice articulating edge. We tried to design a solidbody guitar that had all the advantages of a hollowbody—the ability to feed back in just the right way."

The Red Special is a masterpiece of inventive domestic craftsmanship. The source of the spring in the vibrato tailpiece was a motorcycle kickstand, while the oak body came from a 500-year-old fireplace mantel. The massive neck—Brian's got big hands—contributes to the Red Special's trademark warm sustain. So does the unique switching system that May designed for the instrument's three single-coil Burns pickups. Each pickup has its own on/off switch and phase switch, making it possible to effect a broad spectrum of tones.

"It's very well-suited to that violin sort of tone that I use to build up 'guitar orchestras,'" says May. "That sound was a dream from childhood—I could hear it in my head." Having aced the guitar problem so early on in life, May isn't about to trade the Red Special for any other instrument. "I figure it's gonna last just about as long as I do—with any luck."

photo by kevin westenberg

paul mccartney's
HOFNER 500/1

THANKS TO ED Sullivan and Paul McCartney, the Hofner 500/1 is among the most well-known instruments in history. This is the bass McCartney used at the height of Beatle-mania, not only in the studio but during the group's tours of Japan and America, in the films *A Hard Day's Night* and *Help!* and, of course, on "The Ed Sullivan Show." Affixed to the side of the bass is the set list from the band's performance at Shea Stadium in 1965.

That the venerable Hofner company (founded in 1887) made its reputation building violins, cellos and upright basses is reflected in the appearance of this instrument. Light-weight and hollow-bodied, the 500/1 has but a 30-inch scale length. This bass originally had a pickguard, removed by McCartney at some unknown date.

This was actually the second Hofner that McCartney owned; he used an earlier-style 500/1, which had both of its pickups mounted towards the neck, on the early Beatles sessions ("Love Me Do," "Please Please Me"). McCartney apparently received the second 500/1, which had a neck-and-bridge configuration, as a gift from Selmer, the English distributors for the German manufacturer Hofner.

rick nielsen's
CUSTOM HAMER STANDARD

LONG BEFORE ELECTRIC guitars with custom graphics became a staple in hard rock music, Cheap Trick's Rick Nielsen was tearing up arenas with this all-mahogany 1978 Hamer Standard. This is certainly the most legendary of Nielsen's many custom guitars, and it remains very much on active duty.

"I recorded 'Dream Police' with this guitar, and I still use it every night on that song," Nielsen says. "If you look at it closely, it's beat from playing on it. But if you think about it, I only play it on one song a night, so for it to get so beat up proves that I really *play* the thing. I don't believe in pampering my instruments."

The guitarist's celebrated obsession with the checkerboard motif that adorns the Standard did not develop overnight. "I was associated with that design way before I got this guitar," Nielsen says. "I used to have checkerboard guitar straps that were actually camera straps—and because I played the guitar down at my ankles, I used to have to take two camera straps and sew them together. Then I had some checkerboard pants made.

"After that," Nielsen continues, "I went to Hamer and said, 'I'd like a checkerboard guitar. How are we gonna do this?' They ended up going to 3M and devising some tape to do the job. I don't know what the actual process was, but they did it, and it was one of the earliest graphic guitars to be made. I even had the knobs made so that they would match up exactly with the finish on the guitar when they were turned to where I wanted them to be. I was always a stickler for dumb details like that."

rick nielsen's

GIBSON CUSTOM SHOP FLYING V

"I HAD THIS made at the Custom Shop in Kalamazoo from my '58 V specs—and they added the cool inlays."—Rick Nielsen

rick nielsen's

HAMER DOUBLENECK "UNCLE DICK"

THIS DOUBLENECK MONSTER, pictured on the cover of Cheap Trick's 1983 album *Next Position Please*, is named "Uncle Dick," after its bow-tied owner. Not surprisingly, the guitar's design is the product of a child's imagination. "There was a contest held in Japan back in 1979 where little kids sent in guitar designs," says Nielsen. "And I got the idea of building a guitar that looked like me from one of those entries, but we didn't end up really using it. Then, after a couple of years, I decided that it might be a fun thing to do. So this guy Scott Stephenson, who was working with Hamer at the time, drew up a couple of designs, and this was the one that made me laugh the most.

"The head comes off," he continues. "There's another one of [*Cheap Trick drummer*] Bun E. Carlos. We had them drill a hole in its head so we could put lit cigarettes in the thing. Of course, the guitar is pretty awkward but I just did it for fun—and it's still fun."

Notwithstanding Uncle Dick's obvious value as a novelty, Nielsen is quick to point out that where his guitars are concerned, form is no substitute for function. "It sounds pretty good," he asserts. "When I make these guitars, it's not like, 'Okay, make a cardboard cut-out and I'll play something else.' I want the real thing. You don't want a guitar just for show. I mean, it is for show, but it's got to be able to sound like something."

Thankfully, the guitar has recovered from the "broken leg" it suffered on the *Lap Of Luxury* tour. "I broke the top neck of the guitar once at the Whiskey in Hollywood; I think it happened while we were playing 'The Flame.' The guitar kept cutting out over and over and over, and I just got tired of it. I smashed it through one of my amps, and I actually hit [*guitar tech*] Dave Wilmer. It was very untypical of me. It was just dumb; lack of sleep and lack of brains were responsible. I've done dumb things, but this was *dumb* and it wasn't fun. I was a bad boy."

photo by pitkin studios

Trick
Cheap
HAMER
HAMER

rick nielsen's
HAMER FIVE-NECK

"THIS GUITAR STILL gets more applause than I probably ever will."—Rick Nielsen

ted nugent's
GIBSON BYRDLAND

MOTOR CITY MADMAN Ted Nugent was still a boy when he purchased this guitar from a Michigan music school teacher. "I was only 17 when I bought it in '65. I had a job at a Pemco gas station, and I taught on weekends and played guitar with the Amboy Dukes. It was $712, which you better believe was a good chunk of change back then. My dad thought I was crazy when I asked him to sign for it. He thought I was buying a Buick—a new one!"

Introduced in 1955, the Gibson Byrdland was originally intended for artists who, like co-designers Billy Byrd and Hank Garland, played country guitar with a distinct jazz flavor. Aside from the ES-350T, the Byrdland was the only model in the Gibson line with a 23½-inch scale. This, along with its 2¼-inch hollow body, makes the Byrdland a highly illogical choice for high-volume rock. It's a safe bet that Byrd and Garland never envisioned their namesake instrument used for songs like "Cat Scratch Fever" and "Wang Dang Sweet Poontang."

Ted finds that the Byrdland's unique cedar top creates an "absolutely mesmerizing" tone, and he reports that he used this particular axe, which is pictured on the cover of *Free For All*, at all of his live shows up to 1975 and on every album up to 1980. But the guitar is no longer a member of the Nuge's flock of Byrdlands: "I don't even own it any more. Can you believe that? I sold it to the Hard Rock Café in New York 10 years ago. I'm not a nostalgic guy, but that sure was dumb. I can't believe I did that, but I did. But I still own six. I kept all the best-sounding ones."

berry oakley's
FENDER JAZZ BASS

BERRY OAKLEY USED this Fender Jazz Bass to match musical wits with Duane Allman, Dickey Betts and the rest of the Allman Brothers Band on some of their greatest recordings, including the enormously influential live double album *At The Fillmore East*.

Oakley acquired the bass new in 1969, from a music store in Gainesville, Florida. In his hands, the instrument went through many alterations—most notably the substitution of a 1963 neck for the original. "Berry was always changing stuff on it," says Allman Brothers manager Kirk West. "At one time it had Gretsch pickups in it."

Oakley used this bass until 1971, one year before his tragic death in a motorcycle accident in Macon, Georgia.

photo by kirk west

jimmy page's
GIBSON EDS-1275 6/12-STRING DOUBLENECK

THE CHERRY-RED Gibson EDS-1275 doubleneck 6/12-string guitar continues to be associated with the player who made it famous: Jimmy Page.

The story goes that Page had been attracted to the EDS-1275 ever since he admired a white model on the cover of bluesman Earl Hooker's album *Two Bugs And A Roach*. One thing is certain—he recognized that here was the perfect tool for a player who utilized alternate tunings on stage and wished to minimize guitar changes between numbers.

"I actually got the doubleneck *after* recording 'Stairway To Heaven,'" says Page, "because I needed a single guitar that would allow me to perform the song live." The gigantic popularity of "Stairway," which he'd originally recorded with a Fender Telecaster for the solo and a Fender Electric XII for the 12-string sections, demanded a special on-stage presentation.

Enter the EDS-1275, a doubleneck version of Gibson's popular SG model. Jimmy's was ordered direct from the Gibson factory, then in Kalamazoo, Michigan, sometime around 1971–72. The model was in the regular Gibson catalog only from 1962 to 1966, but Page's special order and very high-profile use of the 6/12 changed all that.

jimmy page's
GIBSON LES PAUL STANDARD

THE LES PAUL Standard's original designers and manufacturers—including Les Paul himself—would no doubt have been shocked by the veneration heaped on this guitar's headstock. Upon its introduction in the early Fifties, it was received with only moderate enthusiasm. But with the coming of the second generation of rock guitarists, the reputation of sunburst Les Pauls built between 1958 and 1960 skyrocketed. Besides Page, other greats who have played these guitars include Peter Green, Dickey Betts, Ace Frehley and Slash.

With the guitar's increase in desirability came a concomitant rise in price on the vintage guitar market. Page paid Joe Walsh *$500* for the classic '59 Standard pictured here. In 1967, one could cruise into the old Dan Armstrong shop in New York's Greenwich Village and stroll out with a tiger-striped '59 Les Paul for $750. Today, similar instruments fetch sums of five figures and beyond.

photo by kevin westenberg

les paul's
"THE LOG"

IN 1941 LES PAUL, working at the Epiphone factory in New York City, built the now-legendary Log, a working solidbody instrument that he continued to tinker with and improve for years to come.

One of the most celebrated guitars ever made, the Log now resides in the Country Music Hall of Fame. At the instrument's core is a 4x4 pine "log," which is surrounded by Epiphone sides. The guitar's back is a piece of plywood fastened to the body with several flathead screws. The instrument's pickups were fashioned from an old electric clock. At 20 pounds, the Log feels more like a wrought-iron girder than a guitar. In fact, it was too heavy for Paul to lug around on tour, but when he did take it to a show, he would wow his audience by removing the sides.

For all the Log's notoriety, its true historical significance is extremely difficult to determine. Contrary to popular belief, the Log was *not* the first solidbody guitar. In fact, at the time it was built, the Vivi-Tone company made a full line of solidbody electrics, and, almost a decade earlier, Rickenbacker had produced a solid Bakelite lap-steel guitar that Paul himself was photographed playing on various occasions. In addition, the Log did not influence later solidbody designs, not even those of the Gibson guitars that sported Les' moniker.

The real explanation for all the buzz about the Log is Les Paul himself. He is, after all, the man whose name adorns one of the most popular guitars ever made. He was also a highly successful recording artist who did much to popularize the electric guitar. More to the point, the guitar he played from 1941 to 1949 on his string of hits, as well as on several Bing Crosby records and on the road with the Andrews Sisters—was the Log.

photo by john peden

les paul's
HALF-SCALE GIBSON LES PAUL

LES PAUL DESIGNED this "mini gold-top" in the mid Fifties so that he could emulate in live performance the high parts he had achieved in the studio by speeding up the recording tape. "The audience would ooh and aah when I walked out on stage with this little baby," recalls Paul. The guitar was fashioned from a single piece of mahogany, with a standard rosewood fingerboard and maple headstock veneer.

The mini design is a remarkable adaptation of the larger-sized models of the same vintage, utilizing such standard Gibson appointments as a scaled-down pickguard and tailpiece. The bridge was cast unusually thin, to complement the low neck angle. The body depth and fingerboard width mirror those of the larger models, as does the single-coil "soap bar," or P-90, pickup.

johnny ramone's
MOSRITE VENTURES II

FEW PAIRINGS OF guitarist and guitar have affected the sound of rock and roll more than Johnny Ramone and this white Mosrite. Ramone's manic brand of distorted, down-stroked power chords was a crucial element of the high-speed playing and three-minute, three-chord songs with which the Ramones almost single-handedly planted the seeds of American punk and laid the foundation of speed metal and grunge.

"I bought this at a used guitar shop sometime around 1978," says Johnny. "I got it to replace my first guitar, which was stolen. That was also a Ventures II model, which was the cheapest of the Mosrites." This guitar was made in the mid-Sixties; a more accurate dating is difficult, as the serial numbers have been filed off.

Despite the guitar's age and years of heavy use, repairs and modifications have been minimal. "When I got the guitar, I removed whatever 'bar thing' it had and put on a straight bridge," says Johnny. "Also, one of the pickups fizzled out, so I had a DiMarzio 'Fat-Strat' put in." In addition, the tone control has been disconnected and wired permanently to the "treble" position, and the tuners have been replaced. The neck, however, hasn't been touched. "They told me it needed a fret job the day I bought it," says the leather-clad guitarist. "And they still say it every time I bring it in for work."

Johnny wears this guitar somewhere around his knees, with the help of two straps that are duct-taped together. "When I first got a guitar, I adjusted the strap where I thought it looked cool, and then I learned to play," he says. "It's important to look cool. That's the reason I bought this guitar, and that's the reason I play it today. Besides, if you play them loud enough, all guitars start to sound the same."

photo by lorinda sullivan

django reinhardt's
SELMER MACCAFERRI

MORE THAN 50 years after he made his greatest recordings, the French-Belgian Gypsy guitarist Django Reinhardt remains unparalleled in the annals of jazz for his sharp attack, remarkable sustain and haunting vibrato.

How did he do it? Sheer genius, of course, had something to do with it. So did the artist's profound romanticism. Finally, there was his guitar. The best American models of the day were unavailable to Django, so he resorted to what was the finest instrument then made in France: the Mario Maccaferri-designed Selmer, the unique tone of which came to be strongly associated with Djanjo.

Mario Maccaferri, a classical guitarist, was hired by Selmer in 1930 to design a new line of guitars. Conscious of the need for loud instruments in those days before amplification, Maccaferri took special care to create a guitar that could project and cut through in an ensemble situation.

The first line of guitars was characterized by a large, D-shaped soundhole, an internal sound chamber, 12 frets to the body and an innovative cutaway body design. Django is often depicted playing this model in early photos. In 1933 Maccaferri was let go by Selmer, and with his departure the company was forced to alter his original designs. Around 1936 they issued the guitar that was to be Django's choice for the remainder of his life. This new instrument dispensed with its forerunner's internal sound chamber, had a smaller, oval soundhole and, most importantly, had 14 frets to the body. The model pictured here has a German-spruce soundboard, rosewood veneer back and sides and a walnut neck with an ebony fingerboard. The hefty 2x4 neck has a slotted headstock and a zero fret and has no truss rod.

After making approximately 1,000–1,200 of these guitars, Selmer discontinued the line around 1940. To hear one in action, pick up any album of material Django recorded in the late Thirties with Stephane Grappelli and the Quintet of the Hot Club of France (the rhythm guitarists are also playing Selmers).

photo by margot reyes

Decca
Django
REINHARDT
(GUITAR)
Stephane
GRAPPELLY
(HOT FIDDLE)
The QUINTET of the
HOT CLUB of FRANCE
LUME 2
HOT JAZZ
THE Quintet
OF THE
HOT CLUB
OF FRANCE
I CAN'T GIVE YOU ANYTHING
BUT LOVE, BABY
SWEET CHORUS
WHEN DAY IS DONE
AIN'T MISBEHAVIN'
RUNNIN' WILD
SOLITUDE
MYSTERY PACIFIC
MISS ANNABELLE LEE
VICTOR HOT JAZZ SERIES
VOL VI

randy rhoads'
JACKSON "V"'s

"RANDY CALLED ME up right after he got the gig with Ozzy and said he wanted to build a guitar," recalls guitar maker Grover Jackson, who was then the president of Charvel Guitars. "He came out to my place with a crude line-drawing scribbled on a piece of paper—and that was the Rhoads guitar. We worked on it that evening, and it took about two months to make the guitar.

"I put 'Jackson' instead of 'Charvel' on the headstock," says Jackson, "because it was the first time we had made a neck-through-body guitar, and Charvel was really known for bolt-on necks. So it was the first 'Jackson' guitar."

Along with the maple through-the-body neck, the prototype guitar has an ebony slab fingerboard, Les Paul-type block inlays, maple wings and a white ivory finish with custom pinstriping. The bridge pickup is a Seymour Duncan distortion humbucker; a Duncan jazz model rests in the neck position. The tremolo is of Jackson's own design.

"Randy liked the guitar very much," Jackson recalls, "but a few months later he called me up and said that he wanted to build another one, because so many people thought it was a Flying V. He wanted something more radical. I worked on it and, a couple of weeks later, he came out with [*Quiet Riot singer*] Kevin DuBrow and looked at the guitar in its wooden state, unpainted. We drew on it for about an hour and decided on a final design. I was going to rough-cut it, just to see what it looked like, but Randy wouldn't watch. He didn't want to know how they were made, because he felt they had a sort of special magic. So he waited in my office, and when I brought it to him he thought it was great. And that was the black guitar."

The streamlined black "custom" has the same maple neck-through-body design and ebony fingerboard as the original "V," with custom inlays designed by Randy and poplar wings. In place of the tremolo is a Tune-O-Matic bridge, with strings coming through the body, V-fashion. The electronics consist of two volume controls, one tone control and a pickup selector.

photo by glen la ferman

keith richards'
JESSELLI ELECTRIC HOLLOWBODY ARCHTOP

ALTHOUGH KEITH RICHARDS is most closely associated with factory-made guitars such as the Fender Telecaster, he also takes a keen interest in supporting the art of custom lutherie. "Sure, it costs some bread," says Keith. "But I think any guitar player who's making some bread should help keep some of the new guys doing custom work alive. If they don't, it could be that another potentially great guitar maker will go down the tubes."

Luthier Joseph Jesselli undoubtedly did not disappoint Richards when he presented him with this beautiful guitar. The carved headstock, with its gold-plated Schaller pegs, is gilded, not gold-painted, and, like the binding around the body, has been antiqued. The slightly curved ebony fingerboard is bound with stepped African elephant ivory, which is pieced together with joints at the ebony dot markers to allow for expansion and contraction. Also made of ivory are the guitar's Art Nouveau-ish inlays, nut and carved end-piece. The custom frets are made of bronze which, unlike the customary silvered nickel, is a self-lubricating material that burnishes with repeated note-bending. The pickups, custom-made by Seymour Duncan, are singlecoils back and front with a stacked pickup in the middle position. The single volume and tone controls are jade knobs with ivory crowns, resting on ebony bases. The three-way ivory toggle that controls front and back pickups, Les Paul-style, is augmented by a pull-knob volume control which activates the middle pickup. The tone control, made by R.A. Gresco, features a limited capacitance system.

The Jesselli guitar certainly cost Keith Richards "some bread." Asked if it was worth it, the Rolling Stone nods his head vigorously.

photo by john peden

robbie robertson's
GIBSON STYLE "O"

WHEN IT FIRST appeared more than 80 years ago, Robbie Robertson's Gibson style "O" must have raised a few eyebrows in what was a conservative world of guitar design. The scroll in the body dates back to Gibson mandolin designs of the 1890's, which were themselves considered by many to be too radical for an American company. This particular guitar was made too early to have a Gibson logo on the peghead, but the rest of its appointments are standard for the model which was made from 1909 to 1924.

The back, sides and neck are all mahogany; the spruce top and back are carved from solid fibers of wood. The fingerboard and bridge are ebony, typical of high-class instruments of the period. The black finish on the top was optional. The pickup wire, secured by masking tape, is, of course, a later addition by Robertson.

The "O" series was based on Gibson's original guitar design and is regarded as the forerunner of the modern archtop guitar. Its sound is much like that of the L-7 (the popular archtop pioneered by Gibson's legendary R&D man Lloyd Loar)—every note explodes but doesn't sustain. The "O" model and, later on, the L-7 were the instruments of choice for players who replaced their banjos with guitars in bands and orchestras.

The long-discontinued and unusually shaped Gibson "O" exudes a distinctly ancient and American air—making it a natural choice for the Americana-loving composer of "The Night They Drove Old Dixie Down."

gary rossington's
GIBSON LES PAUL STANDARD

THIS 1959 LES Paul has been Gary Rossington's primary guitar since the day he bought it in 1971. He's played the sunburst at every Lynyrd Skynyrd concert and on every album from their debut, *pronounced leh-nerd skin-nerd* (1973), through *The Last Rebel* (1992). So close is the bond between the guitarist and this guitar that Rossington finds it nearly impossible to perform without his "baby."

"One day when we were recording *Street Survivors* in Miami," Rossington remembers, "I got lazy and left the guitar on a stand for the night. The next morning, I strapped it on, went to play, and the whole headstock just fell right off—it was connected only by the strings. I started cryin' like a baby. The whole band freaked out; we canceled the day's session and I took off walking. I got about a mile down the road when two friends came by and picked me up. They said, 'What happened back there? Your whole band is acting like they're in mourning—nobody will talk, they're all cryin' and mopin' around.' So I went back, and the studio's maintenance man said, 'I got some glue that can fix that guitar.' And I was like, 'Glue? Man, this is a precision instrument, and it's ruined. You can have it.' I gave it to him, and when I came back the next morning, I went to grab another guitar to play, and he handed me my Les Paul—fixed perfectly."

The headstock is still held in place by the Miami maintenance man's glue job—the only repair Gary Rossington's much-beloved Les Paul has ever needed.

todd rundgren's
GIBSON SG/LES PAUL

THE PSYCHEDELIC 1961 Gibson SG/Les Paul, responsible for what Eric Clapton called the "woman" tone, was purchased by the guitarist in 1966 or '67 after his original sunburst Les Paul was stolen. Shortly afterwards, he commissioned a psychedelic paint job from two Dutch designers, collectively known as The Fool, whose satisfied clients included Jack Bruce and the Beatles.

The SG originally sported a standard red finish and fold-away, side-to-side-action tremolo. At first, Clapton fastened the tremolo unit in place to keep the guitar in tune. He later removed the tremolo in favor of a more stable bridge.

Clapton used the guitar on *Disraeli Gears* and most of Cream's live albums. In 1967 Todd Rundgren saw Cream perform on one of Murray the K's live shows in New York City. There was Clapton, and there was his psychedelic SG. Rundgren was impressed with the guitar, but hardly knew that he would someday own it.

"Eric gave it to George Harrison," recounts Todd, "who gave it to [*British rocker*] Jackie Lomax, who sold it to me in 1974. It was supposed to be a temporary sale. But I didn't hear from him for 10 years, so...."

Rundgren's prize was in terrible condition. "It had a detached wooden bridge—the kind you find on a crappy folk guitar. The paint had worn off the back of the neck, and the wood was like cork. When I took it in for repairs, they said it was going to break off, so they replaced the headstock. I also had to have about eight inches of the guitar below the headstock replaced." Todd subsequently had the guitar repainted and added a stop tailpiece and brand-new knobs.

Todd used the guitar on several tracks with his band Utopia, but leaves it at home these days. "Of course, if I have it in the studio and a guitar player comes in, he's just going to play it."

carlos santana's

CARAVANSERAI GIBSON LES PAUL CUSTOM

THIS EARLY-SEVENTIES Les Paul Custom was purchased new by Carlos Santana to replace the Les Paul he'd played at Woodstock and on the first Santana album (*Santana*). "That earlier one never stayed in tune," he recalls. "At the time, all the equipment was owned by the band, and they didn't want me to buy a new guitar. So I just smashed the one I had and said, 'There, now I *have* to get a new guitar.'"

The Custom's headstock was broken off somewhere along the line and had to be reglued. The instrument, which was originally cherry red, was refinished at some point in its eventful history. Carlos played it on several songs from *Abraxas*, including "Samba Pa Ti," and it was his main guitar for most of the *Caravanserai* album. He also used this axe in Africa at the historic Soul to Soul concert in 1971, where he joined artists like Wilson Pickett and Tina Turner in honoring the mother continent of rock and soul music.

According to Carlos, British blues great Peter Green loved this guitar. Green befriended the Santana band after they recorded and had a hit with his "Black Magic Woman."

"Pete would book a flight and actually follow the band," says Santana. "I guess he was taking a break from Fleetwood Mac. So when we'd play 'Black Magic Woman,' I'd say to him, 'Come on up and jam. It's *your* song, after all.' He always wanted to play this guitar."

photo by michael sexton

brian setzer's

GRETSCH 6120's

BRIAN SETZER WANTED a Gretsch 6120 from the moment he saw a photo of Eddie Cochran, the rockabilly great best known for "Summertime Blues," playing one. "I had no idea what it was called," remembers Setzer. "When I was 17, I saw an ad in the paper: 'Gretsch for sale.' When I found out that it was the same [*kind*] Eddie Cochran played, I bought it on the spot for $100."

Three years later, Setzer and his Stray Cats were sparking a rockabilly revival in England and would soon do the same in America. He made virtually no modifications to the guitar—though he did personalize it with dice and stickers of Fifties pinup girls.

"The stickers and the dice became trademarks, but I put them on without much thought," says Setzer. "I found the pinup girls in an old lawnmower repair shop. And I put the dice on because it didn't have any knobs. I just got a set of Monopoly dice, drilled holes in them, and squirted in some Krazy Glue. My only real modification to the guitar was putting Sperzel locking tuners on; when the band got serious, I realized I had to play in tune. The pickups are stock Gretsch Filter'Trons —they've always sounded fantastic."

After being played night in and night out for several years, the 6120 grew a little the worse for wear, says Setzer. "It had beer spilled on it and smoke blown all over it; it was beat on pretty badly. In about 1984 I ran into Steve Miller in a bar in Germany. We talked about Gretsches and how mine was getting trashed. When I got back to New York there was a big box waiting for me, and to my delighted surprise, it was a 6120 from Steve Miller. And not just a 6120, but a great one!"

photo by sandra johnson

billy sheehan's
FENDER PRECISION BASS

THOUGH BILLY SHEEHAN may play and endorse other bass guitars, he continues to speak lovingly of his "wife"—the Fender Precision that was his devoted companion from his early days with the band Talas right through his co-founding of Mr. Big.

The classic Precision underwent considerable change during Billy's more than three-thousand-gig career. He started customizing it by substituting a maple Telecaster bass neck for the original rosewood one. "It made the guitar sound big, fat and bright," he remembers, "and it was a vast improvement over the original rosewood neck. I got it because I saw Tim Bogert on the *Beck, Bogert And Appice* album holding what looked like a Precision Bass with a Telecaster neck. He later told me it was a reissue of an original Fender bass neck that had a similar headstock."

The Precision also features a stock Fender pickup that is augmented by a Gibson EB-0 bass pickup, installed by Billy to improve the instrument's response on super lows. "I took a chisel, made a hole, and stuck it in. I remember my mom vacuuming the chips off the living room floor." He then ran separate outputs from each pickup into two amps—one to handle the lows from the EB-0 pickup and the other to take the highs from the Fender. "I had two SVT rigs and I sent a pickup into each," he says. "It sounded awesome, plus I was able to do the right mix on the bass by adjusting the volume knobs." Later additions include a Hipshot Bass D-Tuner and DiMarzio custom-wound pickups.

paul simon's
GUILD F-30 NT SPECIAL

NO LONGER OFFERED by Guild, the simple, elegant F-30 NT (Natural Top) Special was popular with folk guitarists in the mid-Sixties for its fine tone and understated appearance. Among those who were seduced by the instrument's charms was Paul Simon, who in 1967 bought two F-30 Specials. Jim Corona, Simon's current production assistant, notes that the first F-30 Special purchased, shown here, was among the singer-songwriter's favorite guitars, "from the day he picked it up at the Guild factory to the day he sent it...to be enshrined at the The Rock and Roll Hall of Fame."

The F-30 Special features Brazilian rosewood sides and back, a spruce top, a mahogany neck and an ebony fingerboard. The neck width at the nut is $1^{11}/_{16}$ inches.

Simon often used his F-30 Special in the studio, notes Corona. "He recorded some of his greatest Simon & Garfunkel hits with this guitar, including 'Bridge Over Troubled Water' and 'Mrs. Robinson.'"

Mark Dronge, currently vice president of DR Strings, was a Guild sales manager when Simon claimed his F-30 Special. "The first thing he did," recalls Dronge, "was play a tune he'd just written—'America.'"

photo by lorinda sullivan

slash's
1959 LES PAUL REPLICA

"I DIDN'T REINTRODUCE the Les Paul," says Slash. "It's been around. I just don't think that anybody who was really popular and touring worldwide was really using Les Pauls around the time Guns N' Roses came out."

Ironically, the guitar that brought the Gibson Les Paul back into the spotlight in the late Eighties is actually not a Gibson at all, but a painstakingly accurate replica of a late-Fifties Les Paul Standard, built by a luthier named Chris Derrig, who died in 1986. Guns N' Roses manager Alan Niven bought the guitar and gave it to Slash during the recording sessions for the band's 1987 debut, *Appetite For Destruction.*

"When I was in the studio doing the basic tracks for *Appetite*," says Slash, "Alan Niven brought this Les Paul for me to use because I was having a really hard time getting a good sound, and I was getting a little frantic at that point because we weren't on the kind of budget—nor did I have the attention span—where we could wait around forever.

"It became my main guitar for a really long time," Slash continues. "And because I couldn't afford a whole handful of them, I took it out on the road for all of Guns' early touring." Slash almost lost his prized possession during one of these early tours: "I had it stolen from me once in the crowd," he recounts. "I was being an idiot, leaning over the audience and getting pulled in, and some guy just grabbed it. I *freaked* once I realized that it was off my person—that I'd completely lost control over it. But our security guys went out and caught the guy before he left the building. That's happened to me a couple of times."

The instrument came with Seymour Duncan Alnico II pickups, which Slash now uses in all of his solidbody, humbucker-loaded guitars, and remains virtually unaltered except for countless pickup rings pulverized by the guitarist during his celebrated onstage antics.

"I don't take that guitar on the road anymore. It's beat to hell, but it still sounds great!"

slash's
GUILD DOUBLENECK

MANY GUITARISTS FIND that switching from an electric to an acoustic and back again on stage is more trouble than it's worth. But Slash is one guitarist who did something about the problem. "I couldn't believe that no one in all this time had come up with an alternative to having a lame acoustic stand at the front of the stage," says Slash. "So I had this idea for a doubleneck acoustic/electric, drew the thing out on a napkin and brought it to Guild.

"It's really a professional guitar. For the average kid playing in his bedroom, it's not really necessary. You do have to have two amps and be able to switch back and forth, because you obviously can't play the acoustic with the same kind of gain as you use for the electric."

The top half of this doubleneck is a hollowbody acoustic with a soundhole and a piezo pickup in the bridge; the bottom is a Les Paul-style electric. Both necks on the guitar have a 24¾" scale, thus duplicating the Les Paul feel that Slash has become so accustomed to.

"It worked out great," the guitarist raves. "It sounds good and it serves its purpose. The most important thing about this guitar is that it's functional—the acoustic sounds enough like an acoustic, even though it's an electric/acoustic, which I don't really go for. It sounds good enough for me to use for every single show during any electric/acoustic song—where previously I would have had to switch back and forth. I use it for 'Yesterdays' and 'Don't Cry'— wherever an acoustic guitar and an electric guitar are necessary, it's really handy. And it's never given me any sort of problem."

photo by neil zlozower

edward van halen's

HOMEMADE ORIGINAL

EDWARD VAN HALEN bought the ash body and maple neck from which he built this guitar from Linn Ellsworth, custom guitar builder and owner of Seattle's Boogie Bodies, in 1975. "It was a junky, crappy body on the bottom of a stack of other bodies," remembers Van Halen. "It was a second. I gave the guy $50 for the body and got a neck for $80. I picked up the two and slapped them together." This bride of Frankenstein, which Edward so casually brought to life, became the celebrated forerunner of the legions of "Superstrats" that were prevalent in the 1980's.

When the bride's body first came into Van Halen's possession, it was pre-routed for three single-coil pickups. Van Halen chiselled a hole to house a humbucker in the bridge position. There he installed a P.A.F. salvaged from a 1961 Gibson ES-335 ("which I had also ruined," says Van Halen); over the years it has been replaced with various humbucking types. The neck pickup (possibly a stock Fender or a DiMarzio) is completely disengaged. The guitar was first sprayed with black and then white Schwinn acrylic lacquer bicycle paint. A black pickguard (also homemade) covered the two front routings. The nut was brass and the bridge was salvaged from a circa-1961 Fender Stratocaster.

This guitar was Edward's main instrument for Van Halen's first several albums and tours. During the band's second worldwide stampede Van Halen replaced the original tremolo with a then-prototype Floyd Rose. Some spirited Van Halen stage antics led to the destruction of that first Linn Ellsworth neck, which the guitarist replaced with "whatever was handy." The Ellsworth neck sported Gibson jumbo frets ("I put those in with the help of some Krazy Glue"). The tuning heads were Schallers. The tone knob pictured here is the original, though the pots have since been replaced.

How did he do it? Edward seems determined to de-mystify his achievement. "There's really no secret. I do what I do through trial and error," says the semi-pro luthier.

edward van halen's
IBANEZ DESTROYER

EDWARD VAN HALEN may be notorious for his use and abuse of hot-rodded Strat-style guitars, but in truth, some of his most popular riffs were recorded with this mid-Seventies Ibanez Destroyer. "I used this guitar for a lot of *Van Halen*. You can hear it on all the stuff that didn't have any whammy bar on it: 'You Really Got Me,' the rhythm track on 'Jamie's Cryin',' and 'On Fire,'" says Van Halen.

According to the guitarist, the Destroyer, which is pictured on the cover of *Women And Children First*, "was one of the few guitars made out of korina wood that you could get without spending an arm and a leg."

Unfortunately, shortly after recording Van Halen's landmark debut, Edward maimed the guitar in a moment of workbench zeal. "It was a great-sounding guitar—until I hacked a chunk out of it to make it look different," he says with a chuckle. "It was ruined! The sound changed from really fat and Les Paul-like to real weak and Stratty. I thought I might have damaged the pickup when I took out the wood, so I stuck in another pickup, but it sounded the same—real bad. The mistake was that I took out a piece right by the bridge, where a lot of resonance and tone come from."

Filled with remorse, Eddie went out and bought another Destroyer. "But by that time," he laments, "they'd changed the body wood."

stevie ray vaughan's
"NUMBER ONE" FENDER STRATOCASTER

Stevie Ray Vaughan's "Number One" Stratocaster was a composite guitar, consisting of prime parts taken from several vintage Strats. This was a blue-collar instrument, with the kind of well-worn appearance that comes from years of use in smoky taverns as well as giant arenas.

The main components of Stevie's "Number One" were a '59 sunburst body and a '63 neck fitted with large frets. The guitar featured a black pickguard, with vintage pickups and pots. Finally—perhaps in an attempt to get a more Hendrix-like feel to the vibrato bar—Stevie at some point had a left-handed bridge unit installed.

Although this was a meat-and-potatoes guitar—distinctly unglamorous—it became an extraordinary vehicle of expression in the hands of the gifted musician who made his statement on it.

On July 9, 1990, just weeks before Vaughan's tragic death, the neck of this Strat was destroyed in a freak stage accident. The neck was pieced back together, and the guitar was buried along with the man who made it Number One.

SRV
Custom

stevie ray vaughan's
NATIONAL DUOLIAN

ONE OF THE most powerful things about *In Step*, Stevie Ray Vaughan's last recording with Double Trouble, is the album's cover image: a seated Vaughan, playing a National steel guitar with great intensity. Since Stevie Ray was hardly known for his acoustic playing, one might assume that the National was simply a prop. Not so, says Rene Martinez, who served as Vaughan's guitar tech from May 1985 until the blues artist's death in 1990.

"This guitar was one of Stevie's favorites," says Martinez. "We took it on the road all the time, and Stevie would use it to try out new material or just to play around."

Martinez says he first saw the National, a 1930's Duolian model, at Vaughan's house in 1985. The instrument's metal body is colored gray-green, with a round mahogany neck that a previous owner had refinished dark brown. The neck joins the body at the fourteenth fret; the headstock is slotted.

Vaughan played bottleneck on the Duolian. "The first day I saw him with it, he pulled out his slide and ripped off some tremendous licks," says Martinez. "That cover of *In Step* says it all. He would pick up the National, tilt his head down and play into the night."

photo by james bland

ron wood's
ZEMAITIS "METAL-FRONT"

TONY ZEMAITIS DOESN'T build your average guitar, but then, his is not your average clientele—unless you consider Keith Richards and Rich Robinson (Black Crowes) to be average. The biggest Zemaitis booster of all, though, is Ron Wood, who has spent much of his Rolling Stones tenure with one of these metal-fronted beauties slung coolly from his shoulder.

For this, his second Zemaitis guitar, Wood asked the luthier to abandon his usual glued-neck, Les Paul-inspired design in favor of a bolt-on neck construction. Zemaitis was more than happy to oblige—sort of. "Actually, that's not a bolt-on," says Zemaitis. "That was a joke—I just made it look like that to make him happy. I do things properly. I don't even think that he knows about it."

In addition to the *faux* bolt-on design, this guitar differs in several other ways from the luthier's usual fare: the body shape does not sport the usual Les Paul contours, and it has three humbucking pickups, selected by push-buttons, instead of the usual two linked by a two-way toggle switch. The circular engraved metal front "has a treasure island map on it. Ronnie would ask for maps depicting the Stones' lifestyle and tours. He had quite a good sense of humor," says Zemaitis.

The luthier, who describes himself as "a little long in the tooth," recently gave up trying to keep up with the insatiable demand for his instruments, and now builds only about 10 guitars a year. There was a time, however, when Britain's rock elite bought his guitars by the truckload. "I remember one Christmas Eve when I was still in London, Ronnie Wood, Ronnie Lane and Rod Stewart came and bought every guitar in the bloody shop. I thought it was a joke for 'Candid Camera,' and I was looking for the camera. But it was no joke."

acknowledgments

THE EDITORS WISH to thank the following people for their invaluable contributions: Tony Bacon and Paul Day, for their expertise and permission to reprint photographs of guitars that appear in their books *The Rickenbacker Book* (Miller Freeman, 1994), *The Fender Book* (Miller Freeman, 1992) and *The Gibson Les Paul Book* (Miller Freeman, 1993); Bill Rich and all at Pitkin Studios, for permission to reprint photos that appear in *Guitars of the Stars, Volume 1: Rick Nielsen* (Gots Publishing Ltd., 1993); John Peden, for his exceptional photographic contributions; Chris Albano and Jon Eiche at Hal Leonard, for their untiring vigilance; Peter Yates, for his impeccable artistic direction; Seymour Duncan and Judy Buchanan, for their time; George Gruhn, for his encyclopedic knowledge of all things guitar; and the Rock and Roll Hall of Fame and Hard Rock Café, for access to their wonderful collections of famous guitars. Most of all, we'd like to thank the many great guitarists who were kind enough to allow their instruments to be photographed for *Guitar World* and this volume.

Thanks also to all the photographers, without whose fine work this book would not have been possible: James Bland, Jay Blakesberg/Retna, Nigel Bradley/Balafon, Harry De Zitter, Sandra Johnson, Glen La Ferman, Mike Graham, Mark Leialoha, Andrew Long, Aldo Mauro, Catherine McGann, Paul Natkin, Karjean Ng, John Peden, Anne Petty, Stephen Pitkin, Margot Reyes, Bill Rich, Sue Schaffner, Michael Sexton, Miki Slingsby, Lorinda Sullivan, Ann Summa, Kim Tonelli, Kirk West, Kevin Westenberg and Neil Zlozower.

Finally, thanks to Stanley Harris and Dennis Page, Publisher and Executive Publisher of *Guitar World*, respectively; Associate Publisher Greg Di Benedetto; and Managing Editor Alan Paul.

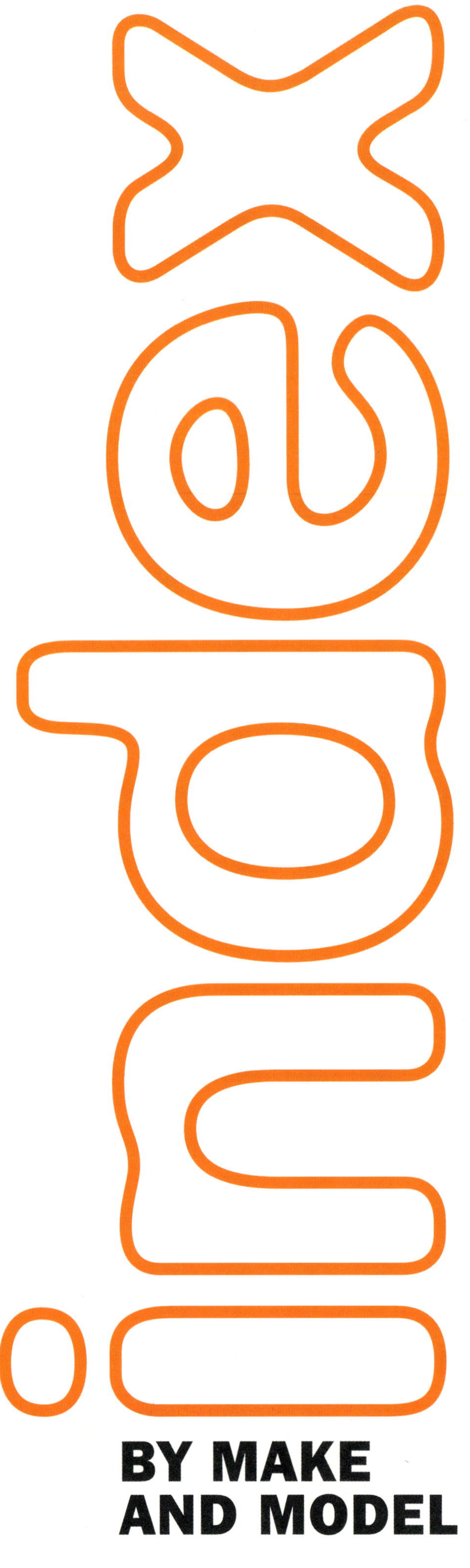

BY MAKE AND MODEL